Wm. B. Burford

Mexican Coffee and Rubber Company

Incorporated under the Laws of Indiana

Wm. B. Burford

Mexican Coffee and Rubber Company
Incorporated under the Laws of Indiana

ISBN/EAN: 9783337059781

Printed in Europe, USA, Canada, Australia, Japan

Cover: Foto ©Suzi / pixelio.de

More available books at **www.hansebooks.com**

Mexican Coffee and Rubber Company

*Incorporated under the Laws
of Indiana*

HOME OFFICE: 29 FITZGERALD BUILDING

INDIANAPOLIS, IND.

INDIANAPOLIS ·
WM. B. BURFORD, PRINTER AND BINDER
1898

..Officers...

W. D. OWEN, President,
Secretary of State of Indiana.

O. W. BUTT, Vice-President,
Capitalist, Kansas City, Mo.

HENRY A. LUCE, Secretary and Treasurer.

...Directors...

J. YORBA,
City of Mexico.

A. B. INGALSBEE,
City of Mexico.

W. D. OWEN.

O. W. BUTT.

F. L. TORRES.

MANUEL L. DE GUEVARA,
Coatzacoalcos.

CHARLES F. LUCE,
Logan, Iowa.

FRANK L. TORRES, Manager of Plantation.

..Board of Control..

HON. THOMAS TAGGART, Chairman.

HON. A. C. DAILY.

HON. U. Z. WILEY.

WM. B. BURFORD.

HON. JESSE OVERSTREET.

H. E. ROSE, General Agent,

29 FITZGERALD BUILDING,   INDIANAPOLIS, IND.

Board of Control...

The by-laws of the Mexican Coffee and Rubber Company provide for a Board of Control, whose duty shall be to have a committee of its members visit Ubero annually, and at any time on the request of the majority of the investors, and make examination into the management of the plantation, comparing its development and general husbandry with that of like plantations on the Isthmus. This examination is to extend into the plantation of each investor, covering the number of trees planted, coffee, rubber, banana and pineapple, and the particular condition of each plantation, and report the same to the full Board. This report will then be printed and a copy mailed to each investor.

Many of our investors will visit their holdings from time to time. Others will probably not visit their plantation until the end of the contract term. From the reports made by the visiting investors and also by the Board of Control, every investor will be constantly in touch with his holding and will be almost as fully posted in it as if it were continually under his own observation.

The interest of the Board of Control is a common one with the investors, and no member of that Board owns a dollar of stock in the Company. It is our experience that investors on the development plan, on the Isthmus, often increase their holdings after a visit to the plantation.

Board Membership...

Hon. Thomas Taggart is a business man of wide experience and one of the best known citizens of Indiana.

A. C. Daily is Auditor of State.

Wm. B. Burford is the well-known printer and publisher.

U. Z. Wiley is the Chief Justice of the State Appellate Court.

Mr. Overstreet is the member of Congress from the Indianapolis district.

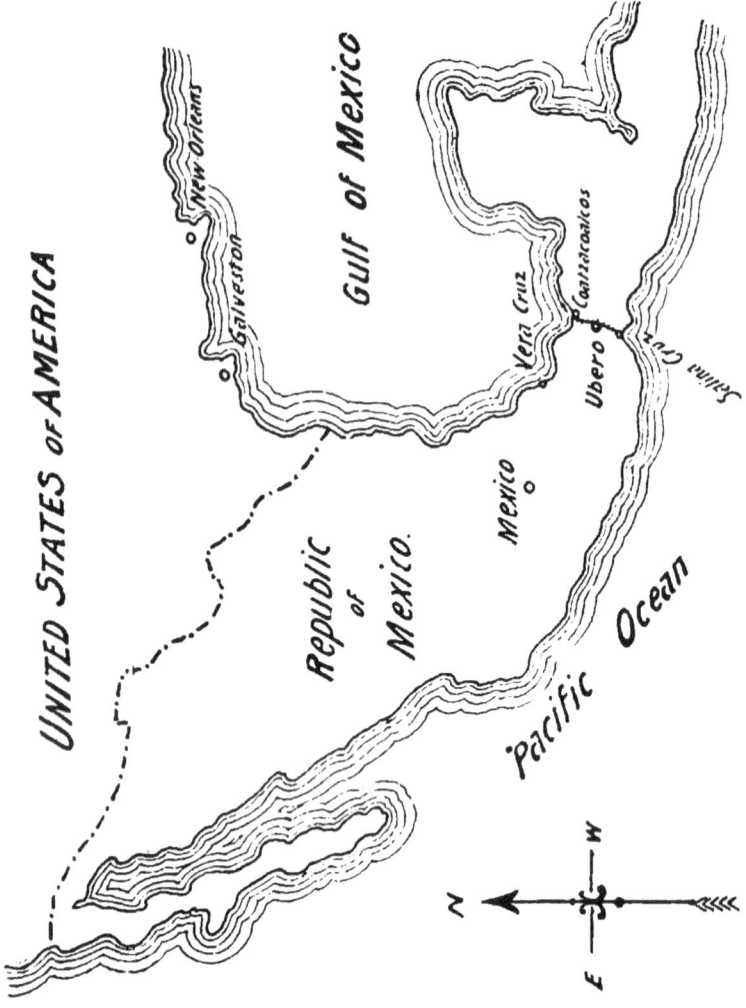

UNITED STATES of AMERICA

Gulf of Mexico

New Orleans

Galveston

Vera Cruz

Coatzacoalcos

Ubero

Salina Cruz

Republic of Mexico.

Mexico

Pacific Ocean

N
E
W
S

Gulf of Mexico

Coatzacoalcos

R.

R.

NATIONAL

Ubero o

Map of

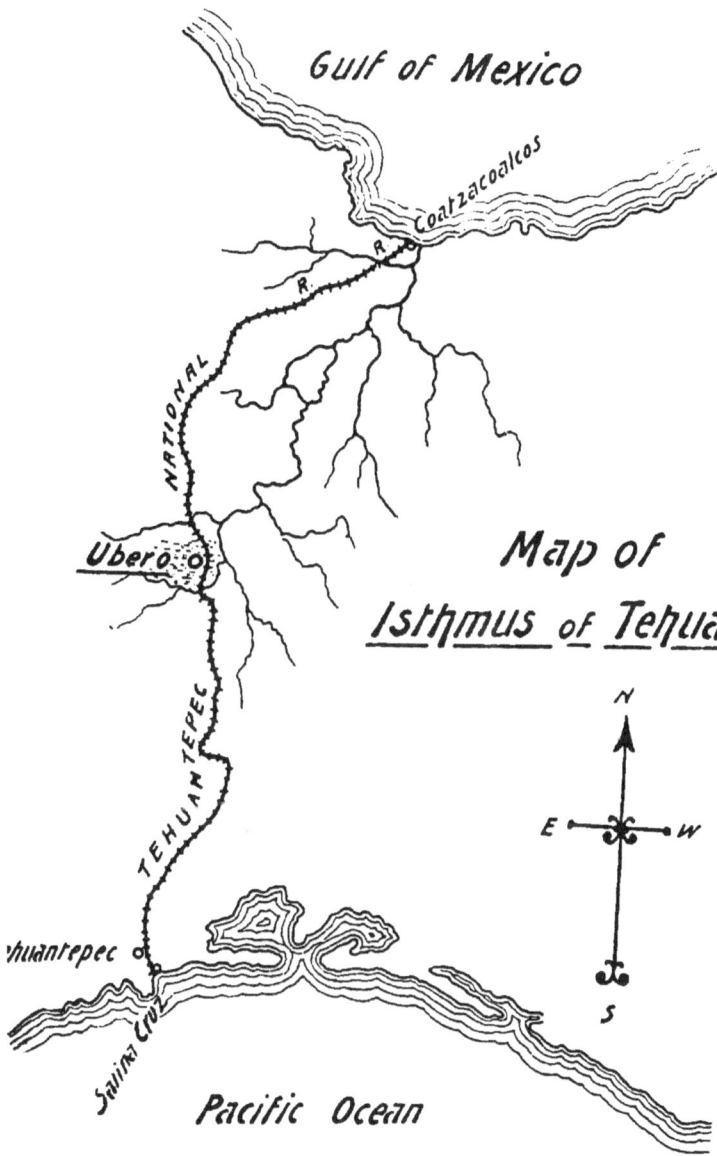

Isthmus of Tehuantepec.

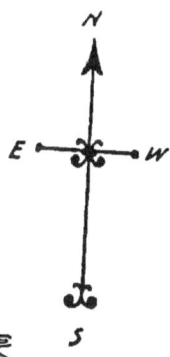

N

E — W

S

TEHUANTEPEC

Tehuantepec o

Salina Cruz

Pacific Ocean

The Awakening

of a Nation....

The Republic of Mexico lies south of the United States like a golden wedge between the Gulf and the Pacific Ocean, dowered by a measureless value of soil and climate and precious stones. When the victorious soldiers of Cortez swept and pillaged through the halls of the Montezumas' they found a magnificence of luxury and a gorgeousness of wealth unknown to Castile and Leon. Two hundred miles north of the City of Mexico, the territory spreads over three thousand square leagues, an arid waste, but its broken mountain sides and rugged gorges for centuries yielded precious metals with a hand so lavish that the cities and homes of the Aztecs rivaled Solomon in his glory.

South of the City of Mexico begins the sub-tropics. A series of rolling hills and valleys irrigated by streams of water pure as crystal sweeping through a soil fertile as the plains of the Jordan three thousand years ago, and the richest and most productive soil on the globe to-day. Three hundred miles down this tapering waste of the continent is found the Isthmus of Tehuantepec, where the extremes of the thermometer are 56 and 98, where fever has never been known to enter, where the water is sweet as a mountain spring, where the soil is five to fifteen feet deep, where rain descends like refreshing dews from heaven and each succeeding season brings bloom and bud and crop. But Nature, so prodigal in gifts to this country, had a limit to her generosity and narrowed this Nile of America to one hundred and seventy miles width. As the salt breezes of the Gulf of Mexico and the Pacific Ocean play back and forth over this wristlet of the hemisphere, they keep the air pure by their salt breath, while waving mahogany and cedar and pine and rosewood and the perfume of orange and pineapple blossom, and the delicate aroma of budding coffee and ripening vanilla and chocolate, make the air odoriferous as the famous spicelands of the Orient.

Nature's richest gifts are always bound in narrow packages; so Mexico's arid plains are two thousand miles broad, but the land which Cortez found, the garden of the world, is only one hundred and seventy miles wide.

It is related by the historians of Mexico that when their ancient people wandered, homeless and oppressed by invading tribes, their prophet said: "When an eagle shall rest on a cactus in the midst of the camp, there shall you build your city, and it shall be set for the defense of the Nation." Their priest and leader, rising early one morning, beheld an eagle with outstretched wings, facing the rising sun, with a snake grasped in its talons and held aloft in death struggle. The priestly leader quickly trumpeted his camp, and, pointing to the imposing emblem, declared the words spoken by their prophet had found answer. At nightfall, the first stakes of the City of Mexico had been planted, and thereon was built a city destined to change the current of human history. An eagle standing on a cactus and grasping a snake with talons and beak remains to this day the emblem of the Nation.

10

Early in the sixteenth century its rule was overthrown by a Spanish invasion and the people were held in subjection for three hundred years. At last their sleeping prowess was awakened, under the leadership of a priest, who, barefooted, had traveled the nation over and knit her people together by a secret oath which had never been divulged, and on the appointed night signal fires flashed from valley and hill-top over the whole land, and the Mexicans fell on the descendants of their Spanish invaders and slew and drove the oppressors from out of the land.

The nation has been half a century in coming to peace and finding stability, but with it the twelve millions of her people wake to find themselves at the doorstep of the United States, the most advanced and prosperous country on the globe, while they are wearing sandals, plowing with crooked sticks and living in shacks.

Fifteen years ago, with peace and stable government, there came to Mexico the dream of wealth and power. With a wisdom that outreached many of the older nations, her people asknowledged their inability to cope with the progress of the nineteenth century, and threw open the portals of the nation and invited industries and commercial activity to come freely and build a home with them. English and German capitalists availed themselves of this invitation. They constructed a gridiron of railroads throughout the country. They then established a chain of banks, with the parent bank at the City of Mexico. This was followed by the construction of street railways and electric light plants in all the cities having over 15,000 inhabitants. The government was fashioned after the model of the United States, having twenty-seven States, with a Congress and President, and generally all the institutions of our country.

11

They proceeded to follow still further the American ideals by establishing a free school system, furnishing tuition and school-books free to the pupils. While the great nations of the world have been barely holding their own during this period, the Republic of Mexico has enjoyed unparalleled prosperity.

Three years since, President Diaz, whose wisdom and patriotic statesmanship will rank him in history with Washington and Cromwell, completed the Tehuantepec Railroad, crossing the Isthmus from the Gulf of Mexico at the port of Coatzacoalcos to the Pacific Ocean at the port of Salina Cruz. Because of the rich, dense tropical undergrowth, the Isthmus was an almost unexplored land, settlements being confined along the rivers whence natives could convey their coffee and rubber and pineapples to the seacoast by the primitive transportation of a canoe. The opening of this railway, putting the most fertile lands on the continent in electric touch and steam connection with the great march of the world, was like weaving a strand of pearls on a cloth of gold.

Before the railroad was completed Mexico begun to attract the attention of the United States. A people usually of quick perception, we had been laggards in this vineyard and had allowed the Englishman and German to come from across the sea and possess the earliest developments of the country. But the Americans now began to pour into the Republic, securing concessions for manufactories and selecting the most profitable agricultural fields. Two years before the Isthmus road was completed a company of Americans opened up a large tract of land twenty miles from the road by river transportation. They sold out much of this land on what is known as the development plan:

12

that is, the purchaser paid a certain sum per acre for five years, at which time he received a deed for the one hundred-acre tract purchased, and then executed a mortgage for two equal annual payments for the remainder of his indebtedness, reserving the option to pay in cash or permit the company to accept the crops for the two years for the indebtedness, the company having contracted to plant and cultivate a certain number of thousands of coffee and rubber trees and turn the plantation over to the purchaser at the end of five years in good bearing condition.

This proposition solved the difficulty of many Americans having limited means, who sought to have a profitable investment in that country, and yet preferred not to go there and remain the five years necessary to develop a coffee and rubber plantation. These development contracts are now nearing completion. Every investor, without exception, is satisfied with his investment, many of them writing that the promises made of enormous returns will be more than fulfilled. We have therefore decided to offer a specially advantageous investment by opening up our Ubero plantation on the development plan. This plantation is situated on the Isthmus Railroad and at its very center, where every advantage that civilization offers in railroad connections, telegraph, postoffice and all the accompaniments of the industrial life of our own country may be had.

We present this pamphlet for your consideration, for every statement herein made can be verified. The practical man in the planting and development of the plantation above referred to is in charge at Ubero plantation, and the estimates on the products of the soil will be fully realized by our investors.

The opening up of the Isthmus of Tehuantepec offers the

last opportunity for great agricultural investment on our continent. This strip of territory, which is only some twenty miles wide in the section that Nature has adapted for coffee and rubber culture, and which does not altogether contain as much land as four average counties in Indiana, will soon be taken up. Out of its remarkable soil, with its matchless climate, great fortunes are now being reaped and still greater ones lie in its bosom awaiting only the touch of the planter to come forth. The native coffee, and rubber, and pineapple, and orange, that have bloomed and ripened and fallen ungathered, are passing into the control of far-sighted Americans. The Isthmus of Panama, seven hundred miles farther south, with its unfortunate De Lessep's canal and its deadly miasmas, will, in time, be forsaken, and the Isthmus of Tehuantepec, so much in touch with American life and peopled by Americans, will become the highway between the Atlantic and the Pacific.

The Isthmus of

Tehuantepec...

The part of Mexico that offers the most attraction to the intending investor by reason of its soil, climate, location and general desirability, is the Isthmus of Tehuantepec.

It is a strip of land only about 170 miles in width, which separates the Gulf of Mexico from the Pacific Ocean, and comprises the southern portions of the States of Oaxaca and Vera Cruz, and the northern portion of the State of Chiapas.

The delightful climatic conditions that are found on the Isthmus of Tehuantepec are due mainly to its peculiar location and topography. It lies a narrow strip of land between two great oceans, and the mountain chain that extends the length of the American continents is here depressed to its lowest altitude, thus permitting a free circulation of the ocean breezes of the Atlantic and Pacific, which bring a pure healthful atmosphere and an abundance of moisture which is condensed and falls in well distributed rains and copious dews.

As the Rocky Mountain range that forms the backbone of the Isthmus lies very near to the Pacific Ocean, that water-shed is narrow and steep and its rivers are short and rapid.

The Gulf water-shed begins about half way between the center of the Isthmus and the Pacific Ocean, at the summit of the mountain range where innumerable little streams find their source, and flow down through rock-walled canons, out around the foothills of the central section where they unite and form the river Coatzacoalcos, that rolls, a great majestic waterway, through the plains of the Gulf section and pours its waters into the Gulf of Mexico at the port of Coatzacoalcos.

Of this special section, Prescott, in his "Conquest of Mexico," says:

"During the first day, Cortez's road lay through the 'Tierra Caliente,' the land that had been so long waiting the hand of the tiller; the land of the vanilla, cochineal, cacao, then afterwards of the orange, the sugar cane, and coffee—products which, indigenous to Mexico, have now become the luxuries of Europe; the land where the fruits and the flowers chase one another in unbroken circle through the year; where the gales are loaded with perfume till the senses ache at their sweetness, and the groves are filled with many colored birds and insects, whose enameled wings glisten like diamonds in the bright sun of the tropics. Such are the magical splendors of this paradise of the senses."

Eighty-five miles from the Gulf port of Coatzacoalcos, and the same distance from the Pacific Ocean port of Salina Cruz, is located the "La Puerta Estate," of which our property is a part.

"La Puerta" (doorway), being situated at the base of the Oaxaca branch of the Sierra Madre range, comprises the foothills, which by their undulations form a series of small slopes separated here and there by numerous streams, among them the Quince Millas, Doce Millas and Ubero, the most fertile region at the head of the Nile of Mexico.

16

From the river Jumuapa, the country ascends on a gradual rise to the northwest, thereby affording excellent drainage and rendering every inch of the tract suitable for cultivation.

Railroad...

In 1852 a scientific commission under the direction of Maj. J. G. Barnard, U. S. Engineer, surveyed the Isthmus to inquire into the feasibility of a ship railway to connect the Gulf and Pacific Ocean, as proposed by Eads. Later the Mexican government, realizing the importance of such a route, built the National Tehuantepec Railroad, a standard gauge railroad which crosses the Isthmus on this line, connecting the port of Coatzacoalcos on the Gulf of Mexico with the port of Salina Cruz on the Pacific Ocean.

The road passes directly through our tract, thus affording direct communication with the ports of the Atlantic and Pacific seaboards, and placing the products of our plantations at the very doors of the great markets of the world.

Another means of transportation is furnished by the Jumuapa river, that skirts the sides of the tract and empties into the Coatzacoalcos at the northeast corner of the land. This river is an important tributary of the Coatzacoalcos, that magnificent waterway that flows into the Gulf of Mexico at the port of Coatzacoalcos, where it forms the harbor of that enterprising seaport. River steamboats can ascend this river and lie along the banks.

UBERO STATION, located on the Company's land, is another important feature. It is the end of the Gulf division,

17

where the railroad has just completed some forty houses for its employes. All passenger and freight trains stop at this station.

TELEGRAPH SERVICE. The Federal Telegraph and Central and South America cable from Galveston run their wires directly through our lands, thus affording direct communication with the whole world.

POST OFFICE and EXPRESS OFFICE are already established at the Company's Station.

FREIGHT RATES are established by the government, and are much lower than in the States, the through rate from our plantations to New York being 50 cents per one hundred pounds.

Our Lands...

Before purchasing our lands a thorough inspection was made of all the tropical districts, our Messrs. Owen and Torres having spent considerable time in the Republic looking for a suitable tract, one that would combine all the necessary requirements of Soil, Climate, Rainfall, Transportation and Labor supply.

All these were found at Ubero, the northern section of the La Puerta estate, which we purchased.

This tract is easily accessible from any part of the world by means of the port of Coatzacoalcos on the Gulf, and Salina Cruz on the Pacific side, and thence by the Tehuantepec Railway to the Station of Ubero; also by boat from Coatzacoalcos up the river of the same name, and the Jumuapa.

18

Climate...

Of the climate, what shall we say? Or, rather, what may we not say? Not in our own fair California; not in tropical Florida; not in sunny Italy, so noted for its bright skies and mellow atmosphere; not in the wide world has it a rival to fear by any just method of comparison. So slight and so gradual are its changes, so conducive to good health and a ripe old age are its controlling characteristics, so tempting and gratifying are its smiles, that to enter its presence is to become a slave to its charms, to wish that its domains might embrace the broad universe.

From the mountains, which are always clothed in the freshest and greenest verdure, and which are never beyond the easy range of human vision, there descend into the warmer plains and valleys reclining at their feet as if patiently awaiting anticipated favors. the softest, most grateful breezes and most refreshing rains.

Soil.....

The soil along the bottoms is composed of alluvial deposits and on other sections of the tract. of a yellow loam, which has been enriched by decayed vegetable matter until it has become dark, intermixed with a little lime and small stone. friable, containing much organic matter in combination with other fertilizing substances. The general depth is from five to fifteen feet: the hillsides having a gentle slope and covered with rich undergrowth. obviate all possibility of wash or land slips, a most important consideration in profitable tropical cultivation.

19

Temperature..

Owing to the peculiar configuration of the country and the depression of the Sierra Madre range at this point, forming a gap, the temperature is much lower here than is generally supposed. This is caused by the cold air currents, principally from the Gulf, and at times from the Pacific Ocean, which blow the greater part of the day and night. The temperature averages from 74 to 78 degrees, the maximum is rarely 98 degrees, and the minimum 56. Frost has never been known on the Isthmus, nor have the surrounding mountain peaks ever had any snow upon them; even the nights are cool and bracing, and while it is hot in the sun, it is always cool in the shade. The temperature here is as agreeable as in other localities at elevations of two to three thousand feet above sea level.

Health...

It may be presumed that from the geographical position of the country, the climate must be unhealthful; but principally on account of its peculiar topography, its climatic conditions are salubrious. Yellow fever, black vomit and other endemic diseases are entirely unknown. The robust and healthy condition of both foreigners and natives, even on the coast, attest the salubrity of this wonderful region.

Rainfall....

The position of the Isthmus, catching as it does the moisture-laden breezes from both the Pacific and Atlantic Oceans, and the mountainous character of the middle and

20

southern section of it, insure an abundant and steady supply of rain. From May until the beginning of July there are light rains; from July until the latter part of October, very heavy rains; beginning of November to February, light showers; March, April and part of May being warm, dry weather. The rainy season on this section of the Isthmus can always be relied upon with great regularity, which, with the rivers and their tributaries and the heavy dews in the dry season, furnish an abundance of moisture, rendering irrigation entirely unnecessary. The average rainfall is 100 inches and the prevailing wind is from the north.

Taxes....

Taxes are exceedingly light, very much lower than they are in the United States, and are only upon improved property.

In the Arena, volume 16, page 49 (the monthly issue of June, 1896), is an ably written article by Justice Walter Clark, LL. D., entitled "The Land of the Noon-Day Sun." Concerning land taxes in Mexico, Mr. Clark says:

"Another bad feature in the Mexican economic system is, that land pays a very light tax. In some States perhaps none, and in all, very much less than its fair share. As a rule unimproved land pays no tax whatever, with a result that land is held in large tracts."

Title.....

The title to our property is perfect, having passed direct from an old estate and been ratified by the Mexican government. The examinations were conducted and reported perfect by the best authorities in Mexico. Lic. Y. Sepulveda, first secretary of the American Legation under President Cleveland, and a lawyer of prominence; Lic. Luis Mendez, president of the Bar Association of Mexico, one of Mexico's ablest attorneys, and Lic. Joaquin De Cassasus, an attorney of note in land titles in Mexico.

furtber Considerations....

In considering the purchase of a plantation for the cultivation of rubber, coffee, tobacco and other tropical fruits, the question which sooner or later arises is:

Where can we get a suitable man to care for our plantation, who thoroughly understands his occupation?

It is essential that a plantation be cared for by a thorough agriculturist, who understands his work and thoroughly understands the labor in the localtity of the plantation in which he is located, and how to manage this labor with the least friction and at the least cost, and so as to bring the greatest returns to the planter. This is just as necessary as the selection of fertile soil, healthful climate, perfect title and quick transportation facilities.

In this the company is exceptionally well fitted, as all our work will be under the personal supervision of our Mr. F. L. Torres, who for the past five years has been in charge of some of the largest rubber and coffee plantations on the Isthmus, working several hundred laborers. He is thoroughly conversant with tropical agriculture, having devoted the past nine years to its study in Mexico; is a thorough Spanish scholar, as well as speaking in the old Aztec tongues still retained by the Indian laborers.

22

F. L. TORRES INSPECTING RUBBER TREE ONE YEAR FROM NURSERY.

The Tropic's
Best Gifts....

Rubber.....

The rubber tree (Castilloa elastica of Cervantes, olquaquitl of the Aztecs, hule of the Spaniards) is indigenous to Mexico, and is found growing wild principally by the river meadows. The tree is a hardy one and nothing affects it, not even parasites or animals.

Scarcely has any article of commerce so rapidly increased in demand in the past few years as has this staple.

So universal has become the use of rubber-tired bicycles, electrical appliances, motor cars, etc., that factories have sprung up in large numbers in England and in the United States, and the fields of the Amazon and the forests of Africa have been drained to their utmost in vain in search for an adequate supply of rubber to meet the ever-growing demand of the new uses to which it has been put.

Most of the rubber for years has been obtained from the fields of the Amazon by cutting down the tree, thus ruining forever the possibility of more than one crop from the tree tapped. So great has been this destruction that it now takes from five to six months to transport the remaining rubber from the Amazon forests to the seaports. These South American rubber forests are unhealthy, and white planters have never been able to successfully withstand the climate.

The Isthmus of Tehuantepec, Mexico, has a healthful climate, and Americans and Englishmen enjoy living there;

at the same time the decaying mould of centuries of vegetation, the regular rainfall, and continual warm sun have brought about the conditions of a veritable greenhouse, and here the rubber tree grows wild in great luxuriance, and here for many years by chopping down the trees or tapping them in their crude way, Indians have furnished considerable rubber for the New York markets. Energetic Americans and Englishmen have found that, as in all other wild fruits, a better quality can be obtained by cultivation, until at present there are several very large, highly cultivated rubber plantations in the Isthmus.

Coffee......

The history of coffee, while not generally known, is very interesting. Its original home is supposed to have been in Upper Ethiopia, from whence it was introduced into Abyssinia as early as A. D. 875. Its cultivation was introduced by the Dutch into Java, in 1690, and as a rare plant into the Botanical Gardens of Amsterdam, which in time bore fruit. The French King, Louis XIV, having been presented by the magistrates of Amsterdam with a fine coffee plant, caused some sprouts of it to be sent to Martinique, committing its care to De Clieux, a French naval officer. The voyage proving long, the supply of water became low, and all of the plants except one died from lack of moisture. With this one the zealous officer divided his scant allowance, bringing it safely to port, where it afterwards flourished. From this one tree, it is said, the American tropical colonies obtained their seed, and from it was produced the numerous varieties now to be found on the American continent.

COFFEE TREE, FIRST BEARING.

Of the few countries where it grows, the many advantages which the Isthmus of Tehuantepec, Mexico, has over the others in the way of climate, nearness to market, and cheapness of labor and great fertility of soil are making her rapidly become the greatest coffee-producing country in the world. Consequently many fine plantations are coming into bearing in tropical Mexico, and the stranger, viewing for the first time her large and thrifty plantations, is struck with wonder at the amount of her production; yet it must be remembered that coffee trees do not live forever. The average life of a tree is only twenty-five years. The plantations of other old coffee-producing countries are becoming fewer and fewer, as their trees die out from old age or worn-out soil. Each year the multiplication of the inhabitants far exceeds the small number of coffee trees planted on new plantations. So, as the inhabitants of Europe and the United States, Mexico and other civilized portions of the world increase, in nearly the same proportion the consumption of coffee increases, a careful view of the situation will show that it is impossible to produce enough coffee to equal the demand.

There is still upon the Isthmus of Tehuantepec, Mexico, a wonderful opportunity for conservative, enterprising men to make fortunes in coffee, as great as the fortunes which have been made in Guatemala, Java and Ceylon, whose fields are so fast becoming useless with old age and over-work.

When coffee is in its normal condition the Mexican berry brings between 17 and 20 cents per pound. The average cost of producing it is less than 5 cents per pound, leaving a profit of 12 or 15 cents per pound.

A medium grade of washed Isthmus Mexican coffee

brings in the New York markets to-day 16 cents per pound. Deducting the cost of production, gathering, washing, etc., of 5 cents each, the planter for his profit receives 11 cents per pound. In other words, at the present condition of things, a profit of nearly 220 per cent. on the cost of production goes to the planter.

There are very few investments in the States which can equal an investment in coffee culture in Mexico.

The average individual in the United States consumes about nine pounds of coffee a year, while in parts of Europe and Holland as high as twenty pounds per year are consumed each. When we take into consideration the rapid yearly increase of the human race in civilized coffee-consuming countries, and the rapid extension of civilization into uncivilized countries, and the fact that for every tree planted one tree dies in an older plantation, and that while we reasonably expect to produce from six to seven pounds of coffee per tree, owing to our rich soil, favorable climatic conditions and careful management of our plantations (yet in many parts of the mountainous districts, not more than from one to three pounds per tree are produced), and the consumption being from nine to twenty pounds to the individual per annum, we can readily see that there is apt to be a scarcity of coffee-producing lands in the near future, consequently an increase of price, rather than overproduction of coffee.

Pineapples...

The Toltecs and Aztecs knew how to cultivate the pineapple, and when the Spaniards conquered Mexico they found the fruit in the markets of the towns on their way from Vera Cruz to the great Tenochtitlan.

From time immemorial the pineapple has been cultivated in Mexico.

Besides the fruit being very delicious and wholesome, a fine wine and vinegar are made of the juice. The leaf furnishes a fiber of extraordinary strength and fineness, making it even more valuable than the fruit. The fiber is made into ropes, cables, binding twine, thread, mats, bagging, hammocks and paper. A pineapple rope 3½ inches thick can support nearly three tons. A textile fabric as fine and beautiful as silk is made of this fiber, too. It is believed that the fine cloth of various colors used by the upper classes among the Aztecs was made of the pineapple fiber.

The "Esmeralda" and "Verde Madura" pineapples grown on the Isthmus are the finest known to the world, averaging seven pounds, with a small core and no fiber, and as they will come into market in the United States two months earlier than the Florida product, we feel that we are fully justified in expecting a net profit from them of 5 cents each.

31

Bananas...

The first banana was brought into America by a Dominican, in 1516, from the Canaries to Haiti, from whence it was transplanted to the Continent, but the plantain is indigenous to tropical America, and was cultivated by the aboriginal inhabitants long before the coming of Columbus. Before the Spanish conquest, the latter, besides corn, Chili pepper and potatoes, formed the Mexican staple article of diet.

Some fifteen varieties grow in this region and yield enormous crops.

During the past few years large quantities of this fruit have been brought by manufacturers and ground into flour, which for pastry is far superior to that made from wheat.

Planters of Honduras and Nicaragua have in past years made immense fortunes in bananas. With a quality of fruit in every way equal, if not superior, we are more than able to compete with them, due to our exceptional transportation facilities.

Oranges....

It is generally supposed that the Spaniards introduced several varieties of fruit trees into this country, among them, perhaps, the sweet orange. Yet, if one has traveled much in Mexico, after seeing the numerous forests of wild oranges, he inclines to the theory that the "ancients" knew of this fruit and that perhaps it was cultivated before the time of Cortez. However, works treating on the history of old or ancient Mexico do not describe oranges.

Owing to the injury to the orange trees in the United States from frost, the supply has been greatly diminished, and has proven Mexico's golden opportunity. The orange season of Mexico is from the latter part of September to the first of December, thus fitting in between Florida and California, and making Mexico absolute in its season, and with practically no competition in its market.

The Mexican orange is juicy and very sweet, especially those grown on the gulf side. A tree, well cared for, will produce 1,000 oranges to the tree. The orange shipment to the United States from the Republic last year was 425 carloads, and experts report that this year it will increase at least one-third.

Lemons....

Lemons are a sure crop. The Isthmus is their natural home. The lemon was known to the Aztecs long before Columbus discovered America. They are found growing "wild" on our land.

Tobacco....

Tobacco is indigenous to Mexico, the product rivaling that of Cuba. Regions have long been celebrated for their tobacco, and have yielded large revenues to the viceroys and rulers of Mexico for centuries past. Mexican tobacco has a flavor and body that is appreciated by experienced smokers, and is noted for its extremely fine quality, and is much sought after by foreigners. Tobacco can be harvested six months after planting.

33

Experts differ widely as to the net profits of tobacco culture, their estimates ranging from $400 to $1,000 per acre. The best grade of Mexican tobacco is rapidly taking the place of the best Cuban, and large quantities are sold annually in the United States and Europe as Havana tobacco. On the Isthmus it is harvested six months after planting, and yields 1,500 to 2,000 pounds per acre. In the "Cultivation of Tobacco in Mexico," by Lewis Le June, a work published by the Department of Fomento, the author says:

"The chemical analysis made by Mr. Eugene Schretz, engineer of the French Government, has proved that in the States of Vera Cruz and Oaxaca, especially in the Isthmus of Tehuantepec, there exists alluvial lands similar to those of Sumidero, San Louis, San Juan and Martinez; that is to say, the best tobacco lands in the world."

Vanilla....

At the time of the conquest of Mexico the Aztecs used vanilla to flavor their chocolate, and from them the Spaniards learned its use and introduced it into Europe.

The plant is a native of Southern Mexico, where the finest and most perfect pods are produced. It belongs to the orchid family, has a pulpy stem which grows several yards in length, attaches itself to trees, and appears to be but little dependent on the soil for nourishment.

Finest Quality.—The fruit pod is from six to twelve inches long and about half an inch in diameter at its thickest part, dark green in its earliest stages and yellow when finally ripe. When prepared for market it becomes reduced to a quarter of its original thickness, is black in color, and emits a very agreeable perfume. It begins to bear about the end of the third year, and will yield on an average seven thousand pods to the acre.

Cacao.....

The tree that produces the "food of the gods" (chocolate), "cacao" of the Spaniards, is a native of Mexico.

Long before the Conquest the Aztecs and other ancient Mexican tribes used the fruit as one of their alimentary beverages. They prepared a drink called chocolatl by mixing the seeds after having crushed them on the metatl, together with fine corn meal, vanilla ("tlilxochitl") and a species of spices called "mecaxochitl," and those that drank it were a picture of health, preserving handsome and vivid features even to old age. All nations subjugated under the Aztec eagle had to bring, among other valuables, a certain number of bags of cacao to the palace in the great Tenochtitlan as an annual tribute to the Emperor. It was so highly prized among the ancient natives that in trade it was utilized as currency among the lower classes.

Chocolate was first introduced into Europe (Spain) by the Spaniards from Mexico. Portugal followed in the use of it; France and England did not appreciate its full qualities until the latter part of the seventeenth century. After the year 1778 it came into vogue in all the cities of Europe. Its alimentary virtues became more generally known, and Doret, a Frenchman, invented a hydraulic machine to manufacture it on a large scale. Since then all civilized nations have consumed this rich American product of Mexican origin, which up to date is not produced in sufficient quantities to meet the world's consumption.

This tree is found growing wild on our lands. In cultivating, 400 trees can be planted to the acre, which produce two pounds per tree, and is worth about 20 cents per pound at the plantation.

Sugar.....

The cultivation of sugar cane is an important industry in the Republic of Mexico, and no part of that country is probably better adapted to its growth and development than the Isthmus of Tehuantepec. The crop is extremely profitable on account of the large yield and the comparative cheapness of its production. The cane is planted only once in ten to twelve years and requires no irrigation. Some of the Company's land is especially suited to its cultivation. The cane is very rich in saccharine, and does well from sea level to an elevation of 4,000 feet.

The yield of sugar is enormous, reaching as high as 70 tons to the acre, and the extraction therefrom furnishing as high as 220 pounds of sugar to the ton of cane, at a cost for the best grade of about 2½ cents per pound—the entire cost of production and manufacture.

Fruit.....

Mexico is probably, all things considered, better adapted to the growth of a greater variety of fruits than any other country on the globe. On the high table lands are found most fruits grown in a temperate zone, while in the coast country nearly all the fruits known to the tropics grow wild in the forest. Of these, oranges, lemons, limes, bananas, pineapples, guavas, mangoes, cocoanuts, granadas, zapote, dates and figs, can be grown on the Company's lands.

The cultivation of these fruits yields a return which will compare favorably with that of the best fruit districts of California and Florida, with the advantage of cheaper labor, cheaper lands and immunity from frosts and drouths.

Corn.....

Corn is a staple diet of the classes in the republic. The supply has never equaled the demand, and every year sees increasing imports to make up the deficiency. On the gulf slope a crop of corn can be raised every four months, and brings from 50 to 80 cents per bushel. But the dry table lands and mountainous regions of the interior produce but little corn, and there the crop is very uncertain, owing to the hot winds and lack of moisture.

It commonly attains a height of ten to fifteen feet, and grows with such luxuriance that among the natives it seldom receives the attention of cultivation. A stick stuck in the ground, a grain or two dropped in and the earth pushed over it with the foot constitutes the common method of planting; and yet such primitive efforts yield from forty to fifty bushels to the acre.

Vegetables...

All varieties thrive here, and tomatoes, radishes, lettuce, etc., can be secured from the garden every day in the year.

Game......

At the present time a large number of wild animals are found on this land—deer, tapir, wild hogs, wild turkey, the royal pheasant, parrots, as well as monkeys, and a great many kinds of rare birds of brilliant plumage, while the river and streams abound in fish. Just now, this is the hunter's paradise; but the game will soon disappear before the encroachments of civilization.

Timber.....

Chicle (chewing gum), mahogany, cedar, rosewood, ironwood, lignum-vitae, Brazil wood, logwood and many other valuable woods are found on our lands.

....WHY?....

After reading our statements thus far you will probably ask: Why? If this is such a wonderful country and so much money can be made there—*Why*, then, does not all the world rush into the production of coffee on the Isthmus of Tehuantepec? Why? *For the very same reason that you yourself have not done so.* Either it has not been called to your attention, or you would prefer to make less money and live in the United States, or you have not the necessary capital to wait five years for a return and support yourself meanwhile.

But if you could secure some of the immense profits that coffee culture on the Isthmus is bound to yield, and could continue to live in the United States while the plantation was being cared for and brought into a perfect bearing condition, when you could migrate to the land of the Aztecs and there enjoy the easy life and munificent income of a coffee planter: if you could do this without being compelled immediately to invest the large amount of ready cash required to accomplish these results, but instead could pay for it gradually out of your income and at the same time avoid the great risk taken by the *inexperienced* planter, the *isolation* from society and the *toil* and *privation* incident to the life of a pioneer, what then?

The Mexican Coffee and Rubber Company make it possible for you to own a plantation on the most reasonable terms:

First. Because it will not in any way interfere with the working of our own plantation.

Second. Because, without materially increasing the cost or lessening the efficiency of our management, we can properly care for these other properties and thereby reduce the expense of maintaining our own.

Third. Because it enables us to contract at a smaller cost a larger amount of labor.

Fourth. Because it will enable us to get a better price for our crops; the larger the production in any particular district, the more numerous the buyers, who, as direct representatives of big importers in New York, Liverpool and Hamburg, are brought together at our very doors in keen competition.

Fifth. Because the cost of hulling, cleaning and milling our own crops can be reduced by utilizing our plant to handle the output of other properties.

Sixth. Because the Company can make a large and legitimate profit out of the transaction.

Thus it can readily be seen that we derive many direct and indirect advantages, and can at the same time give the investor a better plantation at less·cost than he could possibly secure in any other manner.

We state the above facts in order that our position may be clearly understood and the proposition we offer not looked upon as an experiment for which others are asked to furnish the funds.

We believe any sound-reasoning person can readily see the mutual advantages to all parties concerned and that the interests of the Company and its investors are identical.

Our Proposition

Is to make it possible for one of moderate means to obtain a rubber, coffee or tropical-fruit plantation of from twenty-five (25), fifty (50) or one hundred (100) acres for $105 per acre, on the following terms: Seven dollars per acre payable at the time of purchasing. Seven dollars per acre payable each succeeding year for a term of four years, when the plantation is to be turned over to the purchaser, subject to a mortgage of $70 per acre. This mortgage will be payable in two annual payments, without interest, and due at the end of the sixth and seventh years after date of making the contract. The Company agrees to accept the products of the land for these two years in payment of the mortgage, if the owner so desires.

When the land is turned over to the purchaser at the end of the fifth year, every hundred acres shall have upon it

10,000 rubber trees, 5 years old.

15,000 coffee trees, 5 years old.

10,000 pineapple plants.

2,500 banana plants, all in a healthy, bearing condition.

Each tract of twenty-five or fifty acres will have upon it, respectively, one-fourth and one-half of the improvements of the 100-acre tract.

From a conservative basis, the annual income from a 100-acre plantation can be estimated as follows:

10,000 rubber trees, 2 pounds each, @ 50c	$10,000 00
15,000 coffee trees, 30,000 pounds, @ 10c	3,000 00
10,000 pineapples, @ 5c	500 00
2,500 bunches bananas, @ 10c	250 00
Net total	$13,750 00

41

Again we repeat that the above estimates as to the income from these tracts is in every way a conservative one. While we have figured on a yield of two pounds of coffee from each tree, we confidently expect five pounds or more, for the reason that they will receive from the very start the best of care and be given every advantage in the way of proper soil and high cultivation, such as weeding, shading, pruning, topping and other important and essential features. It must be borne in mind that you are not getting an ordinary Mexican coffee plantation, but one laid out and cared for from the start in the best possible manner by men who have had years of experience in the business.

The lowest cash valuation at this time for such a plantation would be $30,000, and it could readily be sold at that price, and yet costing the purchaser on our plan a cash output of only $3,500, running through a period of five years.

During which time the purchaser is free from the annoyance and worry of an inexperienced planter in attempting to properly start his plantation, and he is also the gainer of the cost of living, which would otherwise be a loss while he is waiting for his plantation to bear.

If the purchaser so desires, he can largely increase his income by making arrangements with the Company, so that an additional number of acres of rubber, coffee trees, pineapples, bananas, vanilla, cacao or oranges can be planted and brought to bearing, whichever seems to him to be of the most profit. After the fifth year, if the owner does not care to give his personal supervision to his plantation, the Company will care for it and harvest and market his crops for 10 per cent. of the net profit.

The experience of coffee growers on the Isthmus has been that good, clean coffee has never sold for less than 16 cents per pound, and that the total cost of caring for, gathering, cleaning, sacking, freighting and other charges is within 5 cents, so we have a handsome margin for any contingency which could arise.

Only two pounds of coffee have been counted upon to the tree, but with our trees started in a nursery and attended to from small plants up, with watchful care and proper weeding, shade and cultivation, planted at least nine feet apart in virgin soil of great richness, we have every reason to anticipate six pounds instead of two pounds to the tree.

Rubber usually brings 60 and 75 cents, instead of 50 cents, and from two and a half to four and a half pounds, instead of two pounds.

The estimated profit of the growers of bananas on the Isthmus is 20 cents per bunch net. We have conservatively placed our estimate at 10 cents a bunch.

The bananas grown on the Isthmus are fine, equal in every way to those of Honduras, Nicaragua and the Bermudas, where the profit averages 25 cents, gold, a bunch. With their use becoming more common in the United States, and we being so much nearer market, and with so much quicker transportation, it will not be amiss to count on as much profit per bunch from ours as is made in those countries farther away.

We have estimated 5 cents for our pineapples. Almost this price is obtained in Florida by the growers for their product. There is a difference of nearly 25 cents in the New York markets in the price of their pineapples and ours. The Esmeralda and Verde Madura pineapples are grown to perfection in this locality, and nowhere are they excelled for size and flavor.

43

One thing must not be forgotten. The investor will not be situated in some mountainous wilderness, where he is away from all connection with the world, depending upon the expensive and unsatisfactory method of carrying his produce to market on the backs of burros; neither is he at some isolated point, at the head of some river, where he must wait until the river is high until he can get his products to market, but he is right upon a railroad and a river, with two means of reaching the boats at Coatzacoalcos, which are bound for New York, New Orleans and London, and with exceedingly quick means and low rates of transportation to these points.

We have telegraph lines at our doors connecting us with all parts of the world, thus enabling us to obtain quick reports of the market prices in New York, London and New Orleans before shipping our goods.

The Company's experience, together with the productions of other plantations in their vicinity, has warranted them in agreeing to accept the crop from off the land in payment of the mortgage, and this fact, together with the bond they execute for the faithful performance and carrying out of their contract, is evidence of their good faith and of the absolute confidence they have in the ability of this land to more than realize the income counted upon.

What People Who Know Say of the Rubber Industry.

In 1892 the British minister to Mexico, Sir Henry Neville Dering, in a report to Parliament on the subjects of general and commercial interest in Mexico, which report was issued during the recess and presented to both Houses of Parliament by command of her Majesty, said of rubber:

"The rubber tree (Castilloa elastica of Cervantes, olquaquital of the Aztecs, hule of the Spanish) is indigenous to Mexico, and is found growing wild along both coasts, below 22 degrees north latitude, from sea level to altitudes running from 12,000 to 15,000 feet, and principally by the river meadows. * * *

"The hule tree belongs to Urticaceae, grows wild from 45 to 50 feet high, and has branches only at its upper section. Has smooth yellow bark; its leaves are six to ten inches long, oval, oblong, entire, thick, smooth, bright green and glossy above. * * *

"The best soil for rubber cultivation is a deep, rich loam, such as is found along the alluvial banks. * * *

"Trees planted with soil, climate and elevation adapted for the culture would produce from five to six pounds of juice the first year they are tapped, which amount is equivalent to two and four-tenths pounds of rubber. This product will gradually increase for the next four or five years, and sells for 50 cents per pound on the plantation. * * *

"Thus 240,000 pounds, the yield of 100,000 trees at the first year's harvest, will bring the planter $120,000, besides the profit obtained for corn, vanilla beans, cacao and bananas raised from side planting. * * *

45

"The net profit on the investment, after deducting the entire cost of the land and all expenses up to the first year's harvest, will be $95,000, and each of the succeeding harvests for twenty-five or thirty years will bring a steady income of over $100,000.

"Mexico affords excellent opportunites for the development of this admittedly profitable trade. * * *

"It will be evident, from what has been stated above, that the comparatively small output of India rubber which Mexico has so far been able to achieve may easily be very largely increased by improved facilities, if they were provided, and by the introduction of British capital and enterprise into a field which has hitherto been quite imperfectly developed. The India rubber trade of Mexico, in fact, resembles other industries of that republic, in that it is really in a condition of infancy at present, and no organized efforts have been made to work it for what it is undoubtedly worth. It is hardly necessary to point out that in all matters of this kind, where the development of the native resources has to be vigorously carried on, the Mexican government may be relied upon to give every assistance and facility. Mexico, by her enlightened policy and the honorable manner in which, through a time of great financial stress, she punctually fulfilled all her obligations, has placed herself at the head of the group of republics which are popularly, if not with strict geographical accuracy, referred to as South America; and it is the gratifying position of enterprises which have to depend upon Mexican productions for their profits that they are not hampered or persecuted by the government, as is the case in the Argentine Republic and Brazil. It may be taken for granted that the Mexican government is fully alive to

46

the advantage, especially at the present juncture, to be obtained from the development of the rubber plantations of the country. The excellent promise of these plantations ought, as affording an unusual opportunity for the erection of an additional barrier against the failure of the world's supply, to be a matter of congratulation to the thousands who in this country are in various ways and in different degrees interested in the unrestrained development of the cycling and kindred industries."

Extract from the Financial News, of London....

* * * "Manufacturers have been forced to seriously consider the position in which they might be placed were the supply of rubber to be exhausted. The great cycling industry of the country, and all the trades more or less intimately associated with it, in which rubber is used, are just now really at the mercy of any strong combination of capitalists who might choose to purchase the existing stock of India rubber and speculate largely in the future. * * *

"The supply of raw rubber is, at best, a fixed quantity. It is really diminishing, but for the sake of convenience it may be considered as stationary. The most strenuous endeavors on the part of native rubber collectors and European and other traders failed to increase it last year, and expansion in the future is the reverse of hopeful. It is true that a contrary belief, based on the imports to the United Kingdom, prevails in certain quarters; but those who maintain that the output of 'wild' rubber increased last year have not carefully studied the statistics. We

47

certainly imported 89,621 cwt. more in 1896 than in 1895; but the United States—the second largest purchaser—in ten months of the same year took 84,821 cwt. less than in 1895. The United Kingdom and the United States together import about 85 per cent. of the world's supply, and although other European countries, notably Belgium, increased imports, the whole, bearing in mind that the United Kingdom bought the bulk of the Belgian rubber supplied the United States with over 5,000,000 pounds, would scarcely balance the United States deficit. The monopolists, indeed, might count on a diminishing output, for the destructive methods of the rubber collectors have made an expansion most improbable, if not impossible. All through the tropical regions they kill the plants and trees, and the slaughter has at length reached almost incredible proportions. Reduced to pounds, our imports last year amounted to 48,290,388. As we received nearly one-half the world's supply, the total output may be roughly stated at 100,000,000 pounds. Estimating one pound of rubber as the average product of every tree and plant tapped, it would be no great exaggeration to say that 100,000,000 trees and plants were killed for their rubber last year. It does not need expert botanical knowledge to perceive that such a state of things cannot continue indefinitely, and that a rubber famine in the near future is much more probable than an increased output.

"In March the stock in London and Liverpool amounted to 2,184 tons, which, at last year's average price, £11 2s. per cwt., might have been purchased for £568,688. The stock of Para on December 31, 1896, was 1,049 tons; of other sorts, 2,016 tons; total stock, 3,065 tons, worth, at the above price per cwt., £711,080. As the increased demand

and rise in the value of Para rubber make it very improbable that the stock of Para was larger on March 1 than at the end of last year. It is pretty safe to conclude that a capital of £1,219,768 would have purchased the whole of the rubber available on the first day of last month. Bearing in mind that manufacturers of rubber goods must buy to execute their orders and that the monthly output of raw rubber averaged last year, roughly, 3,764 tons, of the value of £872,784, it would not be difficult for a financial expert to calculate how much capital would be required to maintain the 'corner' and realize a huge profit at the expense of the rubber industry. Assuming that $2,000,000 would have bought the stock in hand on March 1 and the month's output, the calculation is simple enough. It will be evident that the situation is unsafe, and it behooves rubber manufacturers to make such a 'corner' impossible by combining to grow their own rubber.

"Enough has been written lately of rubber cultivation to show that the profits in Mexico at least would be very great; indeed, 300 per cent. on the capital invested has been talked of as a possible return after five years from cultivating Castilloa elastica in the Republic. This is a return which provides plenty of margin for contingencies.

"Rubber growing is no longer in the experimental stage, as witness the plantation of La Esmeralda in Oaxaca, Mexico, to which further reference is made below. Cultivated India rubber plantations are few, for the reason that, in some degree, like the coffee plant, the India rubber tree requires a long period of continuous cultivation before making any return to the cultivator."

49

Government Reports....

Mr. J. J. Williams, principal assistant engineer of the scientific commission under the direction of Major J. G. Barnard, United States Engineer, in 1852, made a report of the condition of the Isthmus, the following of which is an extract:

* * * "The distribution of plants on the Isthmus differs from that of Mexico in general, insomuch that the vegetation of the loftier table lands is less distinctly marked. On the margins of the Gulf or Pacific Ocean are found the usual plants of inter-tropical shores, and in the middle of the Isthmus are found families which vegetate favorably at elevations below 5,000 feet within the tropics, this occurring not because the elevation is sufficient to warrant the growth, but that the lower level of the Isthmus is cooled much below the average temperature of its latitude by the constant northeast wind, by the great humidity of the northern slope and by the proximity of the lofty table lands and mountain summits which cool the land in their vicinity.

"The mean annual temperature of the Gulf shore of the Isthmus is 81 degrees. The summer heat is that of 12 degrees more northerly in Africa and Western Asia, and the winter heat that of its own latitudes even on large continents. In other words, it has a cooler summer and more moderate winter than similar latitudes, and it is this extreme quality of climate which gives to these lands the beauty and profusion of vegetation with which they are clothed.

"It is on the outside of the limits of the equatorial zone and its productions are those of a tropical zone, which is an advantage this Isthmus possesses over any point further south, lying in the equatorial zone.

"Important in value is the Alphoani elastica, or India rubber tree, which is found in astonishing numbers throughout the forests that skirt the tributary streams. * * *

"In the production of fruits and leguminous plants, the Isthmus perhaps stands unrivaled, and it seems superfluous to enumerate, even incidentally, the different varieties which constitute other articles of food, or those deserving of a special culture and adapted for purposes of exportation. Yet many of them claim particular notice, either for their delicious flavor, abundant growth or the nutritive qualities for which they are distinguished. Among these we find the chico-zapote, lemon-cillo, orange, chayote, cocoanut, lemon, pineapple (sometimes reaching the enormous weight of fifteen pounds), melon, mamey, chiramoya, citron, mango, banana, plantain, guava and pomegranate. * * *

"Of the maize, frijoles, sugar, cocoa, tobacco, coffee and cotton raised on the Isthmus, it is difficult to speak in terms which might convey an adequate idea of the adaptation of the soil and climate to their cultivation or the perfection to which they are susceptible of being brought. * * *

"But when we reflect upon the productiveness of the soil, the salubrity of the climate, and the boundless character of the vegetation of the Isthmus, it is not difficult to see how great must be the reward which would crown the efforts of an industrious planter.

"In conclusion, it is utterly impossible, even at a momentary glance like this, not to be struck with the value of the boundless riches which nature has showered into the lap of the Isthmus; nor can we estimate the changes to be effected or the benefits to result from their gathering, when its soil shall become an emporium of commerce and teem with wealth and abundance. * * *

"Even the outline which we have traced presents but a feeble delineation of the golden harvest which is to be reaped in the future. Nevertheless sufficient has doubtless been said to awaken attention to the natural resources of this favored region and to show beyond question the present and prospective value of that which already exists."
* * *

Of the healthful climate of the central part of the Isthmus, Mr. Williams, continuing in his report, says:

"On the northeastern division of the Isthmus, on the Gulf slope, where the rainy season begins in the middle of June and terminates in November, the district appears to be usually healthy, and it is not uncommon to meet with natives seventy and eighty years of age residing there.

"The central division of the Isthmus is perhaps the healthiest, a circumstance due to its elevation and better drainage."

Extracts taken from a Report to the United States Senate

Of the United States Scientific Expedition to the Isthmus of Tehuantepec, Commanded by Captain R W. Shufeldt, U. S. N., 1872.

"The Isthmus presents every inducement to foreigners—thousands of acres of fertile land to be cultivated, in a congenial climate, and no obstacles or prejudices in the way of religious, social or industrial ideas.

"The soil on the Atlantic plains is a rich alluvial deposit, often twenty feet in depth. This region is generally heavily timbered, but occasionally open, grass-covered plains are met with.

"The soil is remarkably fertile, and if cleared and cultivated, would yield abundantly all the agricultural products adapted to this latitude and climate.

"Coffee of a good quality grows on the Atlantic slope and in the central division. From what we saw of the coffee tree growing in the woods and in the gardens, we came to the conclusion that the soil and climate of the Isthmus are well adapted to its cultivation. We were all surprised to find the coffee of so fine a flavor. It is rather milder than the Java, but in flavor is not inferior.

"The hule or India rubber tree abounds on the Atlantic plains. At the present time only a small quantity of the gum is collected, but owing to a large number of trees in this region and the increasing demand for this substance, the day is probably not far distant when this valuable gum will be raised here in large quantities for exportation.

"The pineapple is of good size and fine flavor, and limes and lemons are often seen growing wild.

"There are as many as fifteen well-known varieties of the banana, some of which are a very superior quality. Like the orange, the best bananas are found on the Atlantic plains and in the central division, and they are ripe at all seasons of the year.

"Oranges grow in all parts of the Isthmus, but those of the Atlantic plain and the central division are the best. On the Isthmus of Tehuantepec there is no frost to blight this crop, as there is occasionally in Florida and Louisiana; nor hurricanes to kill it, as in the West Indies; nor are the northers violent enough on the Atlantic plains to injure it.

"Many of our garden vegetables grow very well in all parts of the Isthmus. We saw lettuce, radishes, tomatoes, string beans, beets and onions growing in the gardens.

"The climate is a healthful one, and it is the boast of the inhabitants of the Isthmus that the yellow fever has never visited them.

"The Indians are found settled over the whole Isthmus. They are of a mild and gentle disposition, very muscular and possess, many of them, wonderful endurance. In color they are lighter than our own Indians, their features are much finer, and the expression of the face is more pleasing."

Extracts from a Report of United States Consul General Thos. J. Crittendon

TO THE UNITED STATES SENATE ON COFFEE CULTURE IN MEXICO.

"Heretofore Mexico has not been considered by our merchants as an enlarged or promising field for coffee production, because producers have not shown much activity in presenting the crop to the market. It is strange to those of us viewing it from the present standpoint and acquaintanceship with the bean, that the Mexican coffee should have remained so long unknown to, and unsold in, our market. Since the government of this country has passed into capable hands, since the country has opened its gates to all home-seeking people, since the world has become assured that financial investments, as well as life and property are safe here, as elsewhere, and a large part of the country is accessible by rail and water, a new life, a greater stimulus, has been given to the production of all kinds of tropical fruits, as well by those 'native and to the manner born' as by thousands of foreigners who have removed to Mexico for agricultural purposes. Mexico has shown its capacity to produce the higher as well as the lower grades of the berry—from the most delicate Uruapan to the rougher and less tasteful grains on the higher elevations—and she must become a greater producer for the markets of the world, shrinking from no comparison with the coffee of Brazil and elsewhere. There are already many agents from New Orleans, New York and San Francisco and Baltimore located in the coffee-producing regions of Mexico, buying larger or smaller lots for their employers in the United States. * * *

"The yield of a tree cultivated in a suitable location produces from two to four ounces of merchantable coffee during the year; the second crop yields twice as much, and the third crop, when it has its full bearing, is double the yield of the previous year, and runs up as high as 1.5 pounds. Of course, this is a fair average given, and in many fertile districts of Chiapas, Michoacan, Oaxaca, Hildago, Guerro and Pueblo official reports give from three to five pounds per tree, in its full growth, and from four years after transplanting upward.

"The tree in some districts lives for twenty years after reaching its full bearing period, maintaining itself in a vigorous state and giving the same yield; but experienced planters assert that after the twenty-fifth year the plant begins to show symptoms of decay, its crop decreasing gradually year after year, and ceasing altogether after the thirtieth year.

"Trees planted at a medium distance apart, having a fine quality of soil, good care from the time of planting, and careful attention with them when seedlings, will yield a good crop at thirty years of age. The longevity of the Mexican tree also greatly depends on the development of the principal root or taproot, and consequently on the depth to which it can penetrate and the fertility of the soil."

"Special conditions exist in the Isthmus of Tehuantepec, inasmuch as the tree can thrive well there in places even lower than it is found in other sections of the coffee belt; evenness of temperature is also a very important factor for the successful growth of the plant and the proper maturity of the seed.

"When the thermometer marks a temperature below 55 degrees F. at any time of the year, the cultivation of coffee should not be attempted, especially with the Java and myrtle kinds; the Mocha can stand more cool weather, but not lower than 50 degrees. * * *"

From Consular Report to United States Government, by James J. Peterson, Tegucigalpa, November 11th, 1893:

"The cost of raising coffee, after the plantation is well established, will not reach the sum of 6 cents (gold) per pound, including all expenses of management, labor, interest, wear and tear of machinery, etc.

"With proper care and attention, coffee trees will produce from 3 to 10 pounds each year."

Translation from French Consular Report of 1892:

"Mexican coffee took the first premium at the Centennial Exposition in Philadelphia. * * * Mexican coffees were given the grand prize at the Paris Exposition. * * * They will take the highest award at the World's Fair in Chicago."

Note.—His prediction has been verified.

London "Times," January 4th, 1894:

"There are many healthy signs of commercial and industrial movement in Mexico. * * * That a part of its territory is suitable for coffee culture is certain. There can be no doubt the future of this business is a promising one."

The following is taken from the London Financial Times:

"It is impossible to read the financial papers of London, Paris and Berlin, without being struck with the steady growth of feeling, that Mexico is upon the eve of a period of great prosperity. The development of her wonderful agricultural resources has also begun, and her exportation of coffee and other products of the soil and forests is assuming very great proportions."

Senor M. Romero, Mexican Minister at Washington, says:

"Where the location of a coffee plantation is judiciously made, and the work carried on intelligently and economically, the profits realized may be safely put at 100 per cent. per annum upon the investment."

The Mexican Herald, of February 7th, 1897, says:

"Still with the great development going on, the industry in Mexico at least is but in its infancy. The profits are still great and not likely soon to fall. If there was a satisfactory margin of profit when coffee sold at 13 cents per pound, what must it now be when the average price is 25 cents per pound? With improved methods, both in cultivation and handling the crop, the profits of coffee must increase rather than diminish, despite the anxiety expressed by some that the business is likely to be soon overdone because of the increased number of investors going into it. That has been the cry for thirty years, and still the business flourishes, and to-day is more profitable in Mexico than it ever was."

From "Railway Revolution in Mexico," published in San Francisco, 1895:

"At present the cultivation of coffee is attracting special attention, and on the eastern slope much progress has already been made. Among the reasons is the extraordinary profit which the production of coffee offers. The cost of its production in Mexico, in general, is between 8 and 10 cents per pound, Mexican money, and it sells at from 25 to 32 cents."

From "Coffee in Mexico, Its Cultivation and Profit," by Joseph Walsh, Philadelphia, 1894:

"Mexican coffee is worth at present 20 to 22 cents per pound in the American market, while the average cost of production is 7 cents. A plantation will pay from 100 to 300 per cent. on the capital invested."

From "Coffee Growing in Mexico," by J. P. Taylor, Mexico City, 1894:

"Twenty-five years may be taken as the average of coffee trees to remain in remunerative bearing."
"Estimates as to the profits vary, but the lowest of them are enormous, something like 100 per cent. profit on the capital employed."

The Mexican Financier says:

"Ten years from now the people who are going into the coffee business in this country will be rich beyond their expectations."

www.ingramcontent.com/pod-product-compliance
Lightning Source LLC
Chambersburg PA
CBHW021636270326
41931CB00008B/1052